CONCRETE

EDITED BY WILLIAM HALL

CONCRETE

ESSAY BY LEONARD KOREN

CONCRETE

r many years, I lived in Waterloo on London's South Bank
d worked in Clerkenwell, north of the river. Twice a day,
assed the National Theatre (120–121). To see this great
ilding throughout the year – on a foggy March morning,
a warm September sunset, even in snow – was an
ucation. Sometimes the large cuboid fly tower by Waterloo
dge could feel dark and looming, sometimes pale and
ating, and sometimes, when the conditions were right,
ll but disappeared in a milky grey sky. Seeing how the
mospheric conditions affected the character of the building
ced me to consider the role concrete played. How could
ople call this material austere or bland or cold? My
perience demonstrated the opposite: concrete was lively
d mutable.

other building material has the scope and potential of
ncrete. It approaches architectural alchemy that the densely
mpacted Truffle (76) is made of the same stuff as the sinuous
eightless roof of Meiso no Mori Crematorium (165). Or that
e softly sculpted Hallgrímskirkja (355) is so closely related to
e hard-edged Government Service Center (37). Consider
chel Whiteread's evocative and ghostly House (318–319)
ainst Barragán's vivid and heroic Satellite Towers (297).
e intricate lace pattern at Nottingham Contemporary (93),
the crusty impression left when the logs of Bruder Klaus
apel (84–85) were set on fire.

proximately 7.5 billion m³ (265 billion cu ft) of concrete are
oduced annually. That equates to 1 m³ (35 cu ft) of concrete for
ery person on earth each year. Almost all buildings of the last
ntury have some concrete component, such as foundations,
d it is found in every country in the world – concrete transcends

culture. Despite its range and ubiquity, many people associate concrete with rain-stained social housing, or banal industrial buildings. Detractors of concrete cite such tired monoliths, and point out the failure of the material. Its economy and speed of production have inevitably led to its use on buildings of poor quality – frequently compounded by substandard design and inadequate maintenance. But concrete cannot be held responsible for all the failures of concrete buildings. For too long, negative associations have dominated the public perception of concrete.

I conceived this book to advocate and celebrate concrete's beauty, efficacy and its incalculable contribution to modern life. Many of the best and most influential buildings of the last century are constructed with concrete, from Le Corbusier's Villa Savoye (331), perhaps the quint-essential modernist structure, to Frank Lloyd Wright's spellbinding Fallingwater (205), and from Oscar Niemeyer's nation-defining Brasília (38, 158–159, 321), to Tadao Ando's exhilarating Church of the Light (223).

Without concrete our built environment and the history of architecture would be woefully bereft. It is time to reconsider concrete and its contribution to architecture. This is the place to start.

William Hall

CONCRETE THOUGHTS

a child, at the seashore, I was enamored of making towers, wns and totems out of sand mixed with water – a precursor or surrogate for, concrete. And so later in life, when it came e to choose a profession, I chose architecture. Like many of architectural-school peers circa 1972, I was enthralled by the ld, brash contemporary buildings that seemed to offer clever utions to rigorous, sophisticated design problems. Most these structures were made of concrete. My knowledge of s ubiquitous material was rather rudimentary: a viscous ze was delivered to construction sites in funny trucks with spinning drums in the back; once poured it coalesced into dense, heavy materiality – quintessential hard stuff.

ring a break from my professional indoctrination, I discovered at the vast majority of the non-architecture-obsessed public d a rather different view of these concrete buildings I so mired. People frequently applied the adjectives 'hostile,' 'ugly' d 'aggressive' to the constructions. It was conceivable that ese buildings – particularly those structures rendered in a -called Brutalist style, which was popular back then – might be rceived as such (in error, of course). Their shapes and forms, d their decorative bits, were typically jagged and edgy. But it as the naked, unadorned concrete that really set peoples' rves on edge. 'Unrelenting stretches of coarse greyness' and epressing soullessness' was how they sometimes described it. is was a regrettable misunderstanding, I thought. Concrete is 1oble material. Its development is one of humankind's greatest hievements. It might not be up there with the discovery of fire demand, but it is greater than the invention of plywood, rhaps even on a par with the advent of steelmaking. Some of story's most magnificent edifices have been fabricated out of s extraordinary substance. The Pantheon in Rome, 2,000 years old and still standing strong and proud, is an elegant case in point. Considering this building, how could anyone honestly dispute concrete's preeminent value, aesthetic or otherwise?

Eventually, I did come to understand how Brutalism's Mannerist exaggerations of form and surface could, indeed, incite uncontrollable primal responses. While concrete surfaces provide an excellent record of a building's fabrication process – the false starts and revisions, the dribbles and scratches, the pits, cracks, discolouration and voids – when it is intentionally roughed up further, as the Brutalists were wont to do, it can strike some as visually assaulting.

In truth, the overwhelming majority of architectural undertakings before and after Brutalism's (alleged) excesses employed concrete in infinitely more sensitive and appealing ways. An international array of talented and energetic architects, many of whom are featured in this book, has used this quint-essential hard stuff to create evocative three-dimensional poetry. Louis I Kahn's Salk Institute for Biological Studies (207) is a superb example. It is a rigorously designed tribute to those time-honoured classical values, harmony and balance. With graceful persistence, a procession of faceted forms projects a sense of infinite possibility – which is programmatically appropriate since the stated function of the facility is biological research. Another master of refined concrete architecture, Álvaro Siza, seems to make concrete rise up from the earth itself, then merge seamlessly with the surrounding sand, rocks and ocean. See his Leça Swimming Pools (167). He makes the boundaries between land and water, the natural and the artificial, disappear. Toyo Ito, in his Tama Art University Library (179), demonstrates that concrete also means lyrical delicacy – a quality that belies the

aterial's phenomenal strength. And Luis Barragán (186, 235 297)
oves that concrete lends itself not only to sublime rhythms
d syncopations, but also to unabashed playfulness. Barragán's
chitecture emphatically announces that concrete need not be
ab, or even grey!

———————

the early 1980s, I commenced an unexpectedly long sojourn
Japan. At the time I was quite certain that my preoccupation
th concrete buildings was over. But I was mistaken. Japan was
oidly becoming a wealthy country. Land prices were sky-
cketing and new building construction was rampant. Foreign
chitects were being flown in from far-flung corners of the
obe with briefs from merchants and cultural institutions to
sign and build architectural masterpieces – quickly. Cost was
 object. On the residential front, new homes were sprouting
 everywhere. Real estate was so expensive that, if you were
tunate enough to possess raw land, or even a ramshackle hut,
u had a diamond in the rough. Banks competed ferociously
loan all the cash you required to erect anything you could
ssibly conjure up.

is is when single-family concrete homes began to proliferate.
eemed very odd to me. Why would anyone want to live in
ortified bunker, in the middle of a culture esteemed for its
traordinary tradition of light, open, wood architecture? When
e first concrete house appeared in my neighborhood,
wever, I was intrigued. I tried peering inside, but to no avail.
ypical characteristic of these structures was their absence of

ground-level windows – or any visible fenestration whatsoever. (Surely they must have had lots of skylights and/or interior courtyards, I surmised.) I began developing theories about the character of the people who commissioned and lived in these abodes.

I knew an illustrator, the scion of an old Tokyo family, who had inherited a charming multi-storied wood building in a burgeoning part of town. It was a wonderful place, but he got it into his head that it was 'old fashioned.' Instead of renovating it, he demolished it and erected a nondescript four-story residence-cum-studio, concrete throughout, in its place. The building wasn't at all interesting. Dull and drab, actually. But it was fashionable. Certainly, I hypothesized, he was chasing fashion.

While out on errands in another part of the city, I caught a glimpse of a really big concrete house within a few hundred metres of a huge printing-factory compound. What an odd juxtaposition: a pristine, windowless home right next to an industrial monstrosity. Who would site their super-expensive domicile there? I took a five-minute detour to check it out up close. Next to the discreetly designed main entrance was a plaque with the resident's name. It was someone of wealth and power I knew through my perusal of the Japanese media. This was Mr X's castle, and he wanted all the world to see it. Mr X was obviously advertising his status and financial wherewithal.

Frankly, I was jealous. When my concrete-induced flights of hypercriticality abated, I realized that I, too, would like to live in a concrete house. How tranquil it must be to live in the middle

35 million people when you are protected by 25 cm (10 in) techno-rock. And the acoustical insulation! Not just from the urban din outside, but from room to room. The idea of radiant-heated concrete floors also seemed marvelous. A stable and constant interior temperature throughout the year? No more freezing feet in winter? After living in a flimsy, uninsulated wooden Japanese house for far too long, wouldn't that be grand?

———————

Should my embrace of concrete houses be so enthusiastic? Concrete is a composite of sand, cement, aggregate (crushed rock or pebbles) and miscellaneous additives. (When used structurally – as bearing walls, floors and ceilings – it also contains steel reinforcing rods.) Cement, the binding agent of this mixture, is mainly lime. In order to get lime you have to cook limestone at over 1,400°C (2,552°F). During this process the limestone releases all of its CO_2. The fuel used to heat the limestone also gives off CO_2. Anywhere from five to seven percent of the CO_2 generated by man every year comes from the manufacture of cement. Fortunately, concrete buildings will molecularly reabsorb much of that CO_2 if they stay up long enough – about 100 years. Quarrying for the rock aggregate, crushing it, then mixing it together with the other elements of the mix creates a lot of dust, that is, air pollution. (There are filters, but…) And the process is a loud one, creating noise pollution. If that isn't enough, look at the world's land-fills. Almost a fifth of all the waste therein is either concrete or concrete by products.

With the foregoing in mind, is concrete a morally acceptable building material? From an eco-friendly point of view there are positives. Limestone happens to be the most abundant mineral on the planet, so it is unlikely we will run out of it in the foreseeable future. And, if well maintained, concrete buildings are quite durable. Theoretically, they don't have to be replaced often, thus they can stay out of landfills. Only the amount of concrete needed for any particular construction project actually gets manufactured; there's little production waste. Additionally, monolithic concrete structures, because of their immense thermal mass, cut down on the energy consumed for heating and cooling their interiors. And they are fireproof.

All materials have issues, obvious or latent, relating to their environmental sustainability. Does concrete rank in the 'better' or the 'worse' column? Perhaps we ought not delude ourselves into thinking any one material is all that more righteous than any other. In the unlikely event that our civilization one day reaches a consensus opinion that concrete manufacturing and use is a nasty and unsustainable practice, so be it. But I suspect that will happen around the same time that capitalism is dethroned, consumerism is banished and seeking comfort in material things is perceived as criminal behaviour.

———

I never did live in a free-standing concrete house. The closest I came was my year-and-a-half occupancy of a sprawling Tokyo apartment complex. Every conceivable surface was covered or clad to disguise the underlying concrete. I assumed this was

hide the material's supposed harshness. To my mind it also
[de]prived me of concrete's atavistic pleasures. Clearly concrete
[ha]s a profound sensual dimension. It offers an array of optical
[an]d tactile sensations that have extended our human sensorial
[ra]nge. Concomitantly, concrete is a bearer of visceral know-
[le]dge about the nature of the man-made world in which we live.

[Du]ring my early adulthood, I used to make annual pilgrimages
[to] a natural hot springs resort nestled in a remote mountain
[go]rge, about 25 km (15½ miles) inland from the Pacific coast
[in] central California. My favourite feature there was the rustic,
[lea]ky steam room perched out over a thermal water source,
[adj]acent to a cold-water creek. The floor was fashioned out of
[wo]od planks, widely spaced so the hot vapors could rise up
[fro]m below unimpeded. An eerie, greenish illumination ema-
[na]ted from the roof, which was made from sheets of translu-
[ce]nt corrugated fibreglass tentatively held in place by thin
[wo]oden rafters.

[In]congruously, the massive supporting exterior walls were made
[of] concrete. Because of the resort's inaccessibility, only non-
[loc]ally available supplies were hauled in. The cement for the
[ste]am room's concrete walls was imported, but the sand, rock
[ag]gregate and water were gathered up from the creek and along
[its] banks. Apparently, not a lot of attention was paid to the purity
[of] these ingredients, and, as a consequence, the concrete began
[to] disintegrate not long after construction. When I rubbed my
[ha]nd against the wall, sandy grit and bits of loose aggregate fell
[int]o my palm. I used these abrasives to scrape the top layers of
[de]ad skin from my arms, legs and torso. Afterwards, slightly raw,
[I l]ay down on a waterlogged bench, closed my eyes and enjoyed
[th]e enveloping sensory information.

The image of the crumbling concrete walls always remained vivid in my thoughts. It was fascinating, but also unsettling, that a material noted for its exceptional strength and longevity could so easily fall prey to bad craftsmanship and warm, moist sulfurous air. It brought to mind the sand structures of my youth that were inevitably defeated by the wind and rising tides. We expect the sand creations of innocents to fall prey to natural forces, but not concrete. Concrete has insinuated itself deeply into our collective subconscious. We rely on its absolute physical integrity to lend solidity and certitude, real and meta-phoric, to our lives. Fortunately, in most circum-stances, our technologists and engineers ensure that concrete is fabricated properly so it can fulfill its psychological mandate. This then allows our artists of place – architects – to concentrate on transforming this viscous ooze into better and better launching pads for our imaginations.

Leonard Koren

FORM

◀ A precisely formed road bridge twists its way across this Austrian river. From a driver's point of view the bridge is unremarkable, but from the water a taut roll somehow accentuates the relationship between the road and the river running beneath it.
Schanerloch Bridge, Dornbirn, Austria, 2005, Marte.Marte Architects

An expanding coiled ramp provides access to floors as well as the grand architectural statement explicit both outside and – as shown here – inside. Wright was enchanted by the seamlessness that concrete offered, describing the building as 'the quiet unbroken wave'. 'Here for the first time,' he wrote, 'architecture appears plastic, one floor flowing into another…instead of the usual…layers cutting and butting into each other.'
Solomon R Guggenheim Museum, New York, New York, USA, 1959, Frank Lloyd Wright

A delicate double helix is the focus of London Zoo's famous penguin enclosure. The relationship between the ramp and the rest of the building illustrates a major appeal of concrete to Modernist architects: the junctions between different elements are imperceptible. Penguin Pool, London Zoo, London, UK, 1934, Berthold Lubetkin

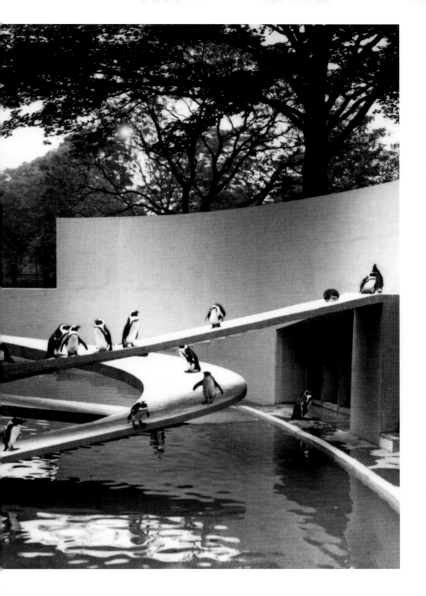

Composed of 152 asymmetrically arranged concrete blocks, this church was designed by notable Austrian sculptor Fritz Wotruba. Wotruba said he hoped to 'form something which shows that poverty needn't mean ugliness'. Considerable local resistance to the building delayed its completion until after Wotruba's death in 1975. Wotruba Church, Vienna, Austria, 1976, Fritz Wotruba

An architectural interpretation of anthroposophy, the spiritual movement Steiner created, the Goetheanum is intentionally liberated from architectural conventions such as right angles and straight walls. The building employs precast concrete blocks to create a faceted and expressive building.
Goetheanum, Dornach, Switzerland, 1928, Rudolf Steiner

◀ Inspired by the heavily tilting ruins of World War II bunkers, the main floor of this church has two planes, both of which are sloped upwards at the edge. Massive concrete walls with rounded edges and slot windows complete the references. Sainte-Bernadette-du-Banlay Church, Nevers, France, 1966, Claude Parent and Paul Virilio

This restaurant sits on the banks of a canal amidst the floating gardens of Xochimilco, a tourist destination in Mexico City. Preferring form to mass, Candela used four thin hyperbolic parabolas to strengthen the combined wall and ceiling of the building. Candela considered it his best work, 'I think it is unsurpassed, and all that a shell should be: simple, graceful, and light'. Los Manantiales Restaurant, Mexico City, Mexico, 1958, Félix Candela

◀ This spare and striking design became a model that travelled around the world. Tensioned steel cables support the saddle-shaped roof. Nowicki's building was completed by William Henley Dietrick after the former died in a plane crash in 1950. Dorton Arena, Raleigh, North Carolina, USA, 1952, Matthew Nowicki

This building is scaled for road vehicles at its periphery, and is of a more inti mate scale around its layered central plaza. Rudolph said of the project, 'I think every curve and line has to have real meaning; it cannot be arbitrary'. The building features Rudolph's signature 'corduroy concrete', a finish developed by the architect. Strips of flat concrete contrast with strips of rough exposed aggregate, disguising the discolouration that can affect concrete. Government Service Center, Boston, Massachusetts, USA, 1971, Paul Rudolph

The Itamaraty Palace houses Brazil's Ministry of External Relations. Visiting foreign dignitaries are received in this grand hall. Lacking handrails, its spiral staircase is stripped to its purest form.
Itamaraty Palace, Brasília, Brazil, 1960, Oscar Niemeyer

◀ This project converted disused factories into a large cultural and leisure centre, comprising theatres, a swimming pool, gymnasiums, a café, restaurants, exhibition spaces and workshops. Two new towers were built and joined at multiple levels by in situ concrete walkways.
SESC Pompéia, São Paulo, Brazil, 1977, Lina Bo Bardi

Torroja was a structural engineer and pioneer in the design of concrete-shell structures. Concrete-shell refers to thin self-supporting structures reinforced with steel. The long cantilevers of these roofs are only achievable using the strength of reinforced concrete combined with the curvature of the forms, which contribute to its structural integrity.
Zarzuela Racecourse Grandstand, Madrid, Spain, 1935, Eduardo Torroja

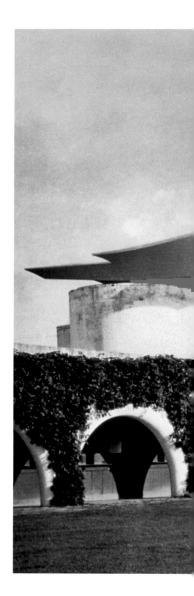

36m (118 ft) wide and 100m (328 ft) long, this aircraft hangar is one of a series built by Nervi for the Italian Air Force. In 1944, the retreating German forces destroyed those that had not already been bombed by the Allies. Nervi's son later reported that his father had been so upset he'd 'wanted to crawl under those hangars and die with them.' Orvieto Hangar, Orvieto, Italy, 1935 (demolished 1944), Pier Luigi Nervi

Built by the lead architect of the United Nations Headquarters, this satisfyingly smooth and featureless exterior belies the large scale of the building, which houses two theatres with a combined seating capacity of almost 1,500. The Egg, Albany, New York, USA, 1978, Wallace Harrison

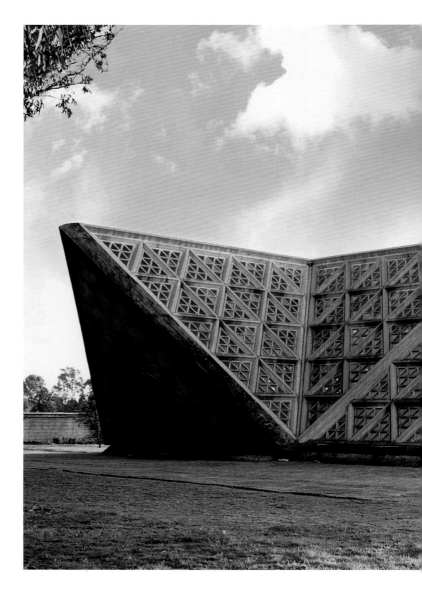

◀ Cruciform in plan, this striking geometric building recalls the Holy Trinity with multiple triangles. The leaning walls are made of a repeating grid of stained glass. Soca Church, Soca, Uruguay, 1963, Antoni Boneti i Castellana

Placed lengthways between two parallel roads, this bus station has a simple visible infrastructure: roads run in one direction, pedestrian access runs perpendicular to the roads, and vertical columns pierce the roof with a tree-like canopy. Jaú Bus Station, Jaú, Brazil, 1975, João Vilanova Artigas

In situ concrete provides both the exterior and the interior finish to this playfully rolled bus shelter. The smaller loop is glazed and encloses a waiting room and café. Bus Station, Casar de Cáceres, Spain, 2005, Justo García Rubio

Concrete is strong in compression (when it is pushed) but weak in tension (when it is pulled). Reinforced concrete uses embedded steel rods to greatly increase the tensile performance of poured concrete. These apartments in Paris, clad in glazed terracotta tiles, form the first multi-level building made with reinforced concrete. The material's strength liberated the floor plans, which have much thinner internal walls than are required in a brick building. The facade is shaped to create a light well, which is normally placed at the back or centre of a building. Rue Franklin Apartments, Paris, France, 1904, Auguste Perret

The long central corridor or 'backbone' of this school was, Botta says, 'modelled like a promenade, with junctions of passages and with indentations that are placed at regular intervals'. An angled concrete roof deflects light from the high windows. Middle School, Morbio Inferiore, Switzerland, 1977, Mario Botta

Approximating a scrunched-up ball of paper, the building has a faceted facade. The architects aimed to challenge conventional linear office buildings and they argue that this building instead 'begins to become an irregular body; out of balance, with many faces in motion'. Oporto Vodafone Building, Porto, Portugal, 2009, Barbosa & Guimarães Architects

'You can make the designs for the exterior architecture, though this won't be a particularly rewarding job for you,' was the uninspiring brief for this building. Designed to verify or falsify Albert Einstein's theory of relativity, the tower houses a vertically mounted telescope and a basement laboratory. Mendelsohn wanted the building to be as special as the science it aimed to corroborate; he created a visionary structure of fluid lines that is without precedent. Einstein Tower, Potsdam, Germany, 1924, Erich Mendelsohn

The dodecahedron used here is a simple geometric structure that can be constructed using 12 identical precast slabs. Torroja wrote, 'In these polyhedral shapes, the play of shadows and light corresponds exactly to the contours determined by the designer. This gives to the shapes a typical hardness and clear-cut outline.' Coal Silo, Madrid, Spain, 1951, Eduardo Torroja

The south coast of England was bombed from the air as early as 1914, prompting the development of early warning systems. A series of acoustic mirrors were built in the 1920s and 1930s. They focused the sound of the air above the English Channel onto a microphone and could detect aircraft up to 32 km (20 miles) away. The mirrors were used until World War II, when the increasing speed of aeroplanes and development of radar made them redundant. The long wall to the left is made of brick. Dungeness Acoustic Mirrors, Dungeness, UK, 1930

Briefed to 'capture the spirit of flight', Saarinen created a building of such futuristic virtuosity that it still looks modern 50 years on. Its flowing, sinuous, aerofoil forms led one critic to describe it as the 'Grand Central of the jet age'. Reinforced concrete embeds a grid of steel rods. In a slab this is a bit like oversized chicken wire and enables gentle rolling curves like those seen here. TWA Flight Center, New York, New York, USA, 1962, Eero Saarinen

This house was built for the architect's sister, then recently widowed, and her two young daughters. Intended to be a therapeutic space, the white interiors were illuminated by narrow skylights along the corridors. U-House, Tokyo, Japan, 1977 (demolished 1998), Toyo Ito

Breuer studied at the Bauhaus and fled Nazi Germany in the 1930s. Because the monks of this monastic community were already resident, Breuer had to employ a 'shadow' planning system whereby new buildings were built adjacent to their predecessors. Subsequently the older buildings were demolished. Saint John's Abbey and University, Collegeville, Minnesota, USA, 1961, Marcel Breuer

The fish, an ancient Christian symbol, was the inspiration for the floor plan of this unusual church. The original design had bricks on the inside and concrete on the outside, but local weather conditions were considered too harsh for the concrete to be used in that way, and the materials were reversed. Ceramic tiles cover the exterior. Kaleva Church, Tampere, Finland, 1966, Reima Pietilä and Raili Pietilä

This egg-shaped shelter demostrates the rarely displayed fragility and delicacy of concrete – qualities that few construction materials can match. Unlike most reinforced concrete that encases steel rods, the Concrete-Pod uses randomly distributed fine steel straws and glass fibres throughout in a material called fibre-reinforced concrete. Concrete-Pod, Nagoya, Japan, 2005, Kazuya Morita

Using earth as a temporary mould, concrete was poured between a room-height stack of hay bales and the earthen framework. When the concrete cured, and the front of the building was sliced off, a calf named Paulina ate away the hay to reveal the room. The remaining nugget seems part of a prehistoric landscape.

Truffle, Costa de Morte, Spain, 2010, Ensamble Studio

◀ Other materials cannot match the scale and textural allure of in situ concrete demonstrated by this curving building. In situ concrete (also called shuttered, poured or cast-in-place concrete) is created by first making a formwork, or frame, of metal or wood, which is then filled by concrete. After the concrete – usually reinforced with steel rods – has cured, the framework is removed. If wood forms have been used they leave an imprint of their grain, as here, and a permanent reminder of the process. Sun Moon Lake Visitor Centre, Yuchih Township, Taiwan, 2010, Norihiko Dan

This former factory building was redeveloped to create a new private gallery space. Thick pre-cast concrete panels clad the building with quoit-sized suckers that are lit dramatically at night. Noppenhalle, Zurich, Switzerland, 2007, Baierbischofberger Architects

Precast concrete panels clad this building with large-scale but subtle patterning. The repeat adds complexity and interest to an otherwise plain series of facades. Pradolongo Housing, Madrid, Spain, 2008, Wiel Arets

◀ A wigwam of tree trunks was the inauspicious beginning of this exceptional chapel in Germany. Then, using a technique called rammed concrete, local farmers laid one 50cm (20in) layer of concrete – between the timber and an outer frame – per month for two years until the walls stood 12m (39 ft) high. Finally, the wood was burnt away to leave a scorched concrete shell.
Bruder Klaus Chapel, Wachendorf, Germany, 2007, Peter Zumthor

A black cube housing a white cube, this gallery contains the national colletion of art of Liechtenstein. The polished walls are of a tinted concrete combined with colourful pebbles from the Rhine Valley and black basalt stone. Aggregate in the form of sand, gravel or crushed stone is an essential and integral part of all concretes because it reduces the brittleness of pure cement.
Kunstmuseum Liechtenstein, Vaduz, Liechtenstein, 2000, Meinrad Morger, Heinrich Degelo and Christian Kerez

A collaboration with the photographer Thomas Ruff saw the entire fabric of this building become a repeat of images. Part minimalist, part Andy Warhol, the dot-screened acid-etched concrete and silk-screened glass facade depicts images from Ruff's collection of historical photographs of German life. Library of the Eberswalde Technical School, Eberswalde, Germany, 1999, Herzog & de Meuron

Situated on a riverbank, this modern but otherwise timeless building contains a sports complex with sports hall, gymnasiums and changing rooms. Tall repeating folds give scale to the long facade. Windisch-Mülimatt Gymnasium, Aargau, Switzerland, 2010, Studio Vacchini

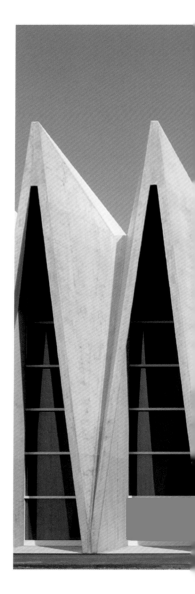

The fluted facades of this art centre feature lace impressions set in precast concrete, referencing Nottingham's nineteenth-century lace industry. As the name suggests, precast concrete is made in a formwork – and often in pieces – off-site, then transported to the site and assembled. This method is often used when more complicated or intricate designs are required.
Nottingham Contemporary, Nottingham, UK, 2009, Caruso St John

This S-shaped curve is one of many residential high-rises in the centre of São Paulo; nonetheless, it remains an icon of the city, symbolic of the economic boom and spirit of progress of 1960s Brazil. The continuous horizontal sun screens offer shade and give the building a strong holistic texture.
Copan Building, São Paulo, Brazil, 1966, Oscar Niemeyer

In a street of upmarket terraced brownstones, Durrell Stone's veil of latticed white concrete bricks provides an unconventional but muted facade to this Manhattan townhouse. Edward Durrell Stone Townhouse, New York, New York, USA, 1956, Edward Durrell Stone

The rain streaks on this wall accentuate the herringbone shuttering of the in situ concrete. The unusually shaped chimneys – actually skylights – were inspired by the fortresses, lighthouses and silos of the neighbouring coastal town of Cascais. Paula Rego Museum, Cascais, Portugal, 2009, Eduardo Souto de Moura

Lampens won the competition to build this church with a traditional scheme but secretly conceived this in situ concrete slab, which was inspired by the jaws of the crocodile that snapped at, but did not kill, a church benefactor in 1570. Lampens made fake development drawings of the traditional church until the real one was a metre tall. By then, with the pastor already on his side, the church board could be persuaded the new design was worth retaining. Our Blessed Lady of Kerselare Pilgrimage Chapel, Oudenaarde, Belgium, 1966, Juliaan Lampens

This 2,000 m² (21,528 sq ft) L-shaped plot contains the mausoleum of Milanese industrialist Giuseppe Brion and his family. Concrete unifies the site, which is composed of a series of spaces with lawns, pools and unusual structures. Scarpa said of the project 'I wanted to show some ways in which you could approach death in a social and civic way'. Brion Family Tomb, Treviso, Italy, 1978, Carlo Scarpa

'Create a silent dwelling for one hun dred bodies and one hundred hearts' was the unconventionally poetic brief for Le Corbusier, whose client, Father Couturier, already regarded him as' the greatest living architect'. Built for a Dominican order of monks, La Tourette gave Le Corbusier the rare opportunity to choose the site. He picked a steep slope with far-ranging views. The building projects from the top of the slope, rather than out of the landscape, and is elevated by columns. Sainte Marie de la Tourette, Lyon, France, 1960, Le Corbusier and Iannis Xenakis

'The concrete block? The cheapest (and ugliest) thing in the building world,' wrote Frank Lloyd Wright regarding the precast elements he used for a series of private houses in Los Angeles. 'Why not see what could be done with that gutter-rat? It might be permanent, noble, beautiful. It would be cheap.' Ennis House, Los Angeles, California, USA, 1924, Frank Lloyd Wright

Housing national treasures in a defensive-looking building, this museum has thick concrete walls, softened by a pixelated pattern, which incorporate small irregular windows. The back of this structure is completely glazed over four stories, while the main exhibition spaces are below ground. Bern Historical Museum, Bern, Switzerland, 2009, :mlzd

This 3,500-capacity sporting arena was built for the 1960 Olympics. Nervi used ferrocement, his own invention. Ferrocement incorporates a fine steel mesh – much finer than conventional rods – in the concrete. It contributes great tensile strength while allowing delicate and flexible forms. Palazzetto dello Sport, Rome, Italy, 1957, Pier Luigi Nervi

Unlike many city markets, San Benito benefits from generous proportions and lots of daylight. In this tall and open space concrete is used for economy and low maintenance. San Benito Market, Mérida, Mexico, 2003, Augusto Quijano Arquitectos

Many of Le Corbusier's buildings for Chandigarh incorporate sun screens and apertures to encourage airflow and diminish the blazing Punjabi sun. The palette of boldly coloured walls offsets the starkness of the grey concrete and reflects the vibrant hues of India, as well as Le Corbusier's own colour theories. Palace of Justice, Chandigarh, India, 1955, Le Corbusier

This beautifully detailed design merges limestone stairs and teak panelling with a brick exterior that matches that of its neighbours. Exposed in situ concrete was used to define this square internal void. 'Exposed' means the concrete was left in an untreated state – not painted or plastered or clad. Phillips Exeter Academy Library, Exeter, New Hampshire, USA, 1971, Louis I. Kahn

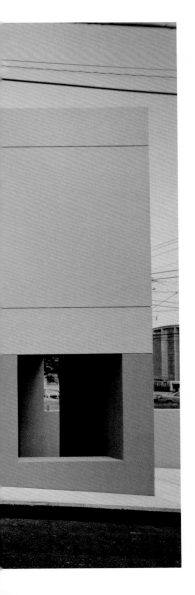

Modern concrete composition has empowered architects to reduce buildings to the purity of line and mass. The cool concrete facade of this immaculate box has two tones. The paler upper floor lightens the perceived mass of the building.
Tetsuka House, Tokyo, Japan, 2005, John Pawson

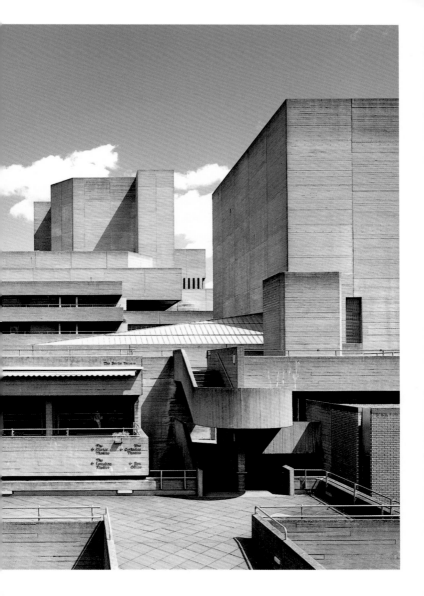

◀ The in situ concrete of this important public building on the South Bank by the Thames has a strong imprint of its timber formwork – a finish that is continued inside. The horizontal terraces are pierced – and the building grounded – by vertical elements housing lift shafts and fly towers. National Theatre, London, UK, 1976, Denys Lasdun

Hundreds of upturned glass tumblers form the circular skylights peppering the ceiling of this luxury Los Angeles home. Concrete is also used for many pieces of furniture, including the sofas shown. Sheats/Goldstein Residence, Los Angeles, California, USA, 1963, John Lautner

Four intersecting but distinct pods make up this curving pavilion and footbridge, which also acted as the entrance to the Zaragoza International Expo. 29,000 fibre-reinforced concrete panels in different shades create a complex 'shark-skin' pattern. Fibre-reinforced concrete uses tiny fibres such as steel, polypropylene and – in this case – glass, to give strength when steel rod reinforcement is inappropriate or unnecessary. Zaragoza Bridge Pavilion, Zaragoza, Spain, 2008, Zaha Hadid

JUXTAPOSITION

◀ The Kaiser Wilhelm Memorial Church was built in 1895 and partly destroyed during an Allied bombing raid in 1943. Eiermann's replacement uses the plaza to unify a series of buildings grouped around the surviving part of the church. Latticed concrete walls encase stained glass squares, colouring the interior by day and emanating blue by night. Berliners have irreverently nicknamed the tower and church the 'lipstick and powder box'. Kaiser Wilhelm Memorial Church, Berlin, Germany, 1963, Egon Eiermann

This collection of massive beams was assembled from precast elements in just seven days. Glass walls enclose the living space, and an 18,000 kg (20 ton) granite block pins the heavy structural elements. Hemeroscopium House, Madrid, Spain, 2005, Ensamble Studio

Inspired by the notion of a living structure that incorporates expansion and change, this public library deliberately appears to be unfinished. The projecting beams reference traditional Japanese timber architecture. Oita Prefectural Library, Oita, Japan, 1962, Arata Isozaki

Two sides of this building allow natural light to filter through its alabaster walls. Four monumental concrete columns are juxtaposed amidst this costly and elegant stone in a vast eight-storey atrium illuminated by a large skylight. This demonstrates how concrete can sit comfortably in the most exalted surroundings. Caja Granada, Granada, Spain, 2001, Alberto Campo Baeza

Attached to a medieval castle these civic offices so challenged the serving mayor that he renounced the building as a 'shattered minaret'. The interior is filled with unusual detailing, cuts and niches (as seen on this staircase) constructed with in situ concrete.

Bensberger City Hall, Bensberger, Germany, 1969, Gottfried Böhm

The Neues Museum on Berlin's 'Museum Island' was built in 1859 and all but destroyed in World War II. David Chipperfield's reconstruction combines different concrete mixtures, demonstrating the variety of characters the material can have. Neues Museum, Berlin, Germany, reconstructed 2009, David Chipperfield

◀ Next to the yellow brick of the original museum, the precast concrete facade of this extension has a ghostly appearance, echoing destruction to the building during Allied bombing raids in World War II. The building has a satisfyingly holistic appearance, while making distinct the new and original parts of the wall. Extension to Museum of Natural History, Berlin, Germany, 2010, Diener & Diener

Constructed around 15 hollow concrete cylinders – each 5m (16 ft) wide – that house the lifts and other services, this building incorporates a newspaper's offices and its printing press, a radio station, and a television studio. Tange developed a flexible modular system that allowed for future expansion of the building. In that sense the building is also incomplete and organic. Yamanashi Press and Broadcasting Centre, Yamanashi, Japan, 1967, Kenzo Tange

The experience of descending the escalators of this boldly industrial-looking underground station is like being part of a massive machine. The lighting, distant rumble of trains and impressive scale add to the sense of drama. Westminster Underground Station, London, UK, 1999, Hopkins Architects

Casa Larrain uses the form of a house that a child might draw, with a pitched roof and simple apertures. But then, one suddenly finds an inverted version of the same thing on top, like a computer programme gone wrong. Severe detailing and materials prevent the concept from being frivolous. Casa Larrain, Los Villos, Chile, 2002, Cecilia Puga

Following a near fatal car accident, the owner of this building became wheel-chair bound: 'Contrary to what you might expect' he told the architect, 'I do not want a simple house. I want a complicated house because it will determine my world.' An office-sized moving platform gave the client access to each floor. Maison à Bordeaux, Bordeaux, France, 1998, OMA

The stratified facade of this community centre signifies its construction with donations of leftover concrete from neighbouring building projects. As well as creating a recognisible and playful building, the design also memorialises the generosity required to create it. SOS Children's Villages Lavezzorio Community Center, Chicago, Illinois, USA, 2008, Studio Gang Architects

◀ These stacked modules were built as dockside residences for an International Expo. Safdie aimed to provide 'privacy, fresh air, sunlight and suburban amenities'. The apartments proved immediately popular and have remained so. The apparently random clusters are carefully contrived to efficiently incorporate services and circulation.
Habitat 67, Montreal, Canada, 1967, Moshe Safdie

Airships are cumbersome and fragile and so need to be kept in hangars during construction and in poor weather. The brief for this pair of 279m (915 ft) long structures stipulated that a spherical diameter of 50m (164 ft) had to fit within the hangar. Additional space was to be avoided, as it would increase costs and building stresses.
Airship Hangars, Orly, France, 1923 (demolished 1942), Eugène Freyssinet

Accessed via a discrete corner staircase, this 12m (39.4 ft) long building houses a laboratory for the study of cosmic rays. Candela used hyperbolic parabolas – the modification from a straight barrel shell increasing its strength – to create a 16mm (⅝ in) concrete roof, the thinnest he ever made. The design allows cosmic radiation to pass through the roof.

Cosmic Ray Pavilion, Mexico City, Mexico, 1951, Félix Candela

This complex fills a difficult site with a group of five buildings. The dominant structure slices across the ground-floor commercial spaces, seemingly into the street. Its sleek deflected plan has a facade without apertures on one side and zigzagging balconies on the other. Corso Italia Apartment and Office Complex, Milan, Italy, 1956, Luigi Moretti

◀ The culmination of a palatial avenue of government buildings, monuments and memorials, Niemeyer's geometric elements have a playful appearance, but their balanced distribution demonstrates masterful judgment. National Congress of Brazil, Brasília, Brazil, 1960, Oscar Niemeyer

Triangular concrete panels wrap this angular building, which is inspired by the river valley it sits in. Its form follows that of a pair of eroded pebbles – each pebble housing a performance space. A city of 11 million residents, Guangzhou is still only the fourth-biggest conurbation in China. Guangzhou Opera House, Guangzhou, China, 2010, Zaha Hadid

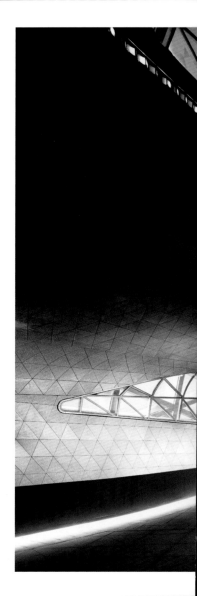

LANDSCAPE

◀ This vast hall is part of an architecture faculty. Vilanova Artigas used wide ramps to link levels, so as to avoid divisions and create an open building with spatial continuity. He said, 'I saw it as a spatialization of democracy, in dignified spaces, without front doors, as I wanted it as a temple where all activities are valid'. Faculty of Architecture and Urbanism at the University of São Paulo, São Paulo, Brazil, 1969, João Batista Vilanova Artigas

This billowing roof sits, in the words of the architect, 'floating above the site like slowly drifting clouds'. Its gentle, calming undulations give the building a subtle presence, entirely appropriate to its role as a crematorium. Meiso no Mori Crematorium, Kakamigahara City, Japan, 2006, Toyo Ito

Architect Álvaro Siza proposed forms requiring only limited excavation, due to budgetary constraints, for these seaside swimming pools. The concrete walls and pavement match the lighter coloured rocks that surround them.
Leça Swimming Pools, Leça de Palmeira, Portugal, 1966, Álvaro Siza

◀ This 60m (196.9 ft) long, droplet-shaped structure is approached via a long wooded pathway with views to the sea. This is a space for sensory contemplation, with large apertures allowing light, rain, wind and sounds to permeate the building and modulate its ambience. Teshima Art Museum, Teshima, Japan, 2010, Ryue Nishizawa

This car factory was built on five levels. Each vehicle rose through the building during production, and emerged completed at the 1,000m (3,281 ft) long rooftop test track. Fiat Lingotto Factory, Turin, Italy, 1923, Giacomo Mattè-Trucco

Prefabricated skateboard ramps can be made from wood, plastic or metal, but concrete has become the predominate material for custom-built skateparks due to the lack of maintenance it requires. For the benefit of neighbours a sound barrier was built into the fabric of the park. To the disappointment of skate-boarders, his cannot be ridden. Skate Bowl at Deer Park, Munich, Germany, 2010, Realgrün Landschaftsarchitekten

A field of austere tombstone-like blocks encourages visitors to roam the rows and remember those killed in the Holocaust. Approaching the centre of the field, the slabs grow taller and less even, creating an unsettling and disorientating effect. Memorial to the Murdered Jews of Europe, Berlin, Germany, 2005, Peter Eisenman

No wall is straight in this suburban Japanese house on a wooded hillside slope. Multiple levels throughout the house correspond with the site's topography. The owners' home office can be seen here overhanging the living space. Y House, Chita-shi, Japan, 2003, Power Unit Studio

The arches of this library differ in width from 2 to 20 m (7 to 66 ft) and seem randomly distributed, but the walls remain an equal thickness, giving continuity in form as well as material and colour. The irregular distribution and scale of the arches allows for different spaces – some are open, some are intimate – by turns promoting interaction or concentration. Tama Art University Library, Tokyo, Japan, 2007, Toyo Ito

Housing the work of just three artists – Claude Monet, James Turrell and Walter de Maria – this subterranean gallery is predominantly lit by a series of skylights that jut out of the landscape. Chichu Art Museum, Naoshima Island, Japan, 2004, Tadao Ando

This narrow, multi-level holiday home sits on an almost impossibly steep site. Exterior stairs rest above those indoors and give access to tiered outdoor spaces. Exposed concrete is coloured to match the massive stones on site. Tolo House, Vila Real, Portugal, 2005, Álvaro Leite Siza

Rejecting the Modernist approach of open park and high-rise structure, Rewal created a series of low-rise layered terraces, courtyards and in-between spaces in a contemporary interpretation of a traditional Indian village. Asian Games Village, New Delhi, India, 1982, Raj Rewal

This vivid composition of walls and water are part of a private estate including a house and stables. Barragán often developed his projects while they were being built. For San Cristóbal, he created temporary cloth walls prior to construction to help envisage the final walls' arrangement, and later used coloured papers on the unfinished structure to ensure the correct blend of hues. San Cristóbal Stables, Mexico City, Mexico, 1968, Luis Barragán

In this unconventional collection of over 200 apartments – some of which have two or three floors – every one is different. The unexpected corners and niches of the building encourage a diverse treatment of space and promote contact between neighbours.
Les Étoiles Housing, Givors, France, 1981, Jean Renaudie

Called Hyakudanen, (hundred-level garden) these terraced gardens are part of a vast complex of buildings including a conference centre, hotel and restaurants. The gardens are built on the site of land that was excavated to build the artificial islands in Osaka Bay, including that of Kansai Airport.
Awaji Yumebutai, Awaji, Japan, 2000, Tadao Ando

◀ This unusual building incorporates shops, homes and offices, but most of all parking. It is not so much a reinvention of the car park as a reinvention of public space generally, like layered public squares in the sky. A central spiral staircase connects the wall-less floors. 1111 Lincoln Road, Miami, Florida, USA, 2010, Herzog & de Meuron

Four tiered seating areas face a recessed open stage in this outdoor public concert hall in the centre of a large public square. A tall overhanging tower provides lighting, while a bar and offices are situated in the spaces beneath the stands. Campinas Cultural Centre, Campinas, Brazil, 1976, Fábio Penteado

Sitting in an excavated 6m (20 ft) deep pit gave this school the impression of a great warship in dry dock. Its position in London's genteel, stuccoed Pimlico area created an unexpected and radical vision. Pimlico School, London, UK, 1970 (demolished 2010), John Bancroft

On the site of a former quarry, this cemetery is embedded in the Catalonian hills. Mourners are led along a winding pathway in a ceremonial descent towards the burial caskets.
Igualada Cemetery, Barcelona, Spain, 1994, Enric Miralles

This 50 m (164 ft) wide flying saucer, perched on the edge of a cliff, was designed when Niemeyer was 89 years old. A wide winding slope connects visitors to the entrance 10 m (33 ft) above the ground. Niterói Contemporary Art Museum, Rio de Janeiro, Brazil, 1996, Oscar Niemeyer

◀ Searching for an architect for the new ministry building, Georgian Minister of Highways George Chakhava decided he was the best man for the job. Suspended above the ground and piled up like a child's game, the structure allows trees to flow around the building. Georgian Ministry of Highway Construction, Tbilisi, Georgia, 1975, George Chakhava and Zurab Jalaghania

Wright took dramatic advantage of a beautiful wooded ravine by positioning this private home overhanging a rushing waterfall. Cantilevered concrete terraces contrast with existing bedrock, which Wright allowed to penetrate the interior, making the integration of building and landscape even more explicit. Fallingwater, Mill Run, Pennsylvania, USA, 1935, Frank Lloyd Wright

One of the most highly regarded scientific research centres in the world, the Salk Institute sits on a cliff overlooking the Pacific Ocean. Founder Jonas Salk aimed to create an environment that would entice the best researchers from around the world. Kahn helped him to choose the site and created something approaching a secular monastery for science. Salk Institute for Biological Studies, La Jolla, California, USA, 1965, Louis I Kahn

Like a giant magnet attracting a box, Bo Bardi's galleries are suspended 8m (26 ft) above the ground, retaining views towards the downtown and a sense of liberation. As Bo Bardi herself describes it, 'I didn't search for beauty. I've searched for freedom.' São Paulo Museum of Art, São Paulo, Brazil, 1968, Lina Bo Bardi

An uninterrupted, undulating floor creates a new type of interior space in this Swiss educational centre. 'The concept was to make one very big room,' explains Ryue Nishizawa of SANAA. 'Standing on top of the hill you might not see the other hill but might hear faint voices. It is like a park.' Rolex Learning Centre, Lausanne, Switzerland, 2010, SANAA

◀ This underground reservoir is built in a public park. Aiming to disrupt the landscape as little as possible, the building is partly submerged in the hill and a grass covering reduces its presence on the landscape. When established, plants will grow around and through the perforated walls, further reducing its impact. Water Reservoir, Basel, Switzerland, 2009, Berrel Berrel Kräutler

This pavilion at the Venice Biennale Giardini communicates the muted coolness of the Nordic countries. Several trees grow through the roof, encouraging visitors to consider the distinction between indoors and out-doors. Nordic Pavilion, Venice, Italy, 1962, Sverre Fehn

◀ Raised off the ground like a visiting spaceship, this otherworldly building houses an interactive science museum. The interior has a flowing, layered floor plan, hinted at by the unusual window arrangement and angled detailing. Phaeno Science Centre, Wolfsburg, Germany, 2005, Zaha Hadid

Built on the site of a disused granite quarry – brought back into service briefly to provide aggregate for the project – this exposed concrete stadium has a capacity of 15,000 seats. The rooftop gutters funnel water into long concrete troughs projecting from the cliff. Braga Stadium, Braga, Portugal, 2003, Eduardo Souto de Moura

Three sides of the building feature grids of sun screens to cool and shade the offices, reflecting the severe climate. An unusual U-shaped roof – an abstraction of a sacred cow's head – tops the main entrance. Parliament Building, Chandigarh, India, 1962, Le Corbusier

LIGHT

◀ A cut cross meets the ceiling, floor and walls of this small residential church with memorable flair. Ando failed to persuade the client that no glass was necessary in the cross itself. Twenty years later he told a lecture hall 'one day I will remove that glass...an architect must never, never, never give up!' Church of the Light, Ibaraki, Japan, 1989, Tadao Ando

The concrete-shell roof of this factory is pierced with glass skylights. Candela developed an umbrella construction – a reinforced concrete stem column and gently curving parabolic planes – to build the lightweight roof. The building survives, but the skylights do not. The current owner filled them in. High Life Textile Factory, Mexico City, Mexico, 1955, Félix Candela

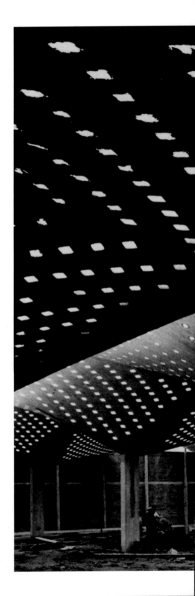

Mushroom-shaped columns support the floors without the use of beams, and the building is wrapped in a 'curtain wall' of glass. In a curtain wall the structure of the building is internal, allowing the exterior walls, often of glass as here, to be hung away from that structure. This avoids the visual weight of columns and load-bearing walls. Boots Factory, Beeston, UK, 1932, Owen Williams

This lofty underground concourse, with undulating ribs of concrete, is so vast it could contain Canary Wharf (Cesar Pelli's One Canada Square) laid on its side. Efforts have been made to retain daylight, so that – even 27 m (89 ft) below ground – passengers on the platform still have a glimpse of the sky.
Canary Wharf Underground Station, London, UK, 1999, Foster + Partners

Unencumbered by heavy stone columns, this church is flooded with light and demonstrates the advantages of reinforced concrete. Perret chose to eschew a conventional cruciform plan, instead returning to something redolent of very early churches – a rectangular plan more closely approximaing a basilica. Notre-Dame du Raincy Church, Le Raincy, France, 1922, Auguste Perret

Le Corbusier's countryside monastery was designed, in the architect's words, 'to give the monks what men today need most: silence and peace...This Monastery does not show off; it is on the inside that it lives.' Indeed, the otherwise brutally grey in situ concrete is brought alive by colour and light in this chapel. Sainte Marie de la Tourette, Lyon, France, 1960, Le Corbusier and Iannis Xenakis

Luis Barragán's use of simple forms, bold colours and filtered light here creates a restrained space with vivid energy that few architects have matched. The case clearly demonstrates Barragán's assertion that the ideal space 'must contain elements of magic, serenity, sorcery and mystery'.
Casa Gilardi, Mexico City, Mexico, 1975, Luis Barragán

The Pantheon's ceiling has been an inspiration to architects and builders for centuries, and remains the world's largest unreinforced concrete span 2,000 years after its construction. The thickness of the dome wall varies from a heavy 1.2 m (3.9 ft) around the oculus – the only source of light – to an incredible 6.4 m (21 ft) at its base. Pantheon, Rome, Italy, 126 AD

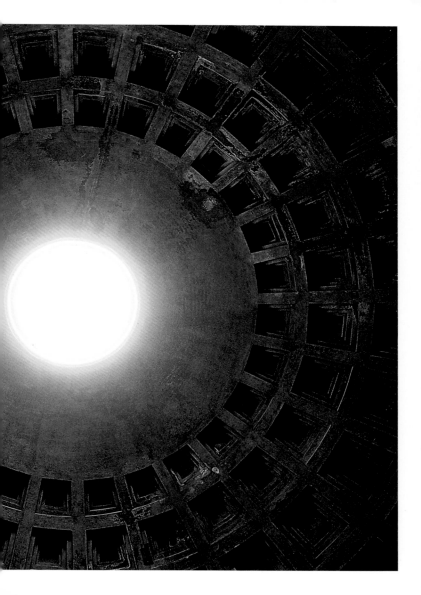

Deliberately avoiding architectural conventions belonging to specific religious denominations, this is a cross-faith space for prayer and reflection situated at the UNESCO Headquarters in Paris. The granite floor came from a building near the blast centre of the atomic bomb that hit Hiroshima. UNESCO Meditation Space, Paris, France, 1995, Tadao Ando

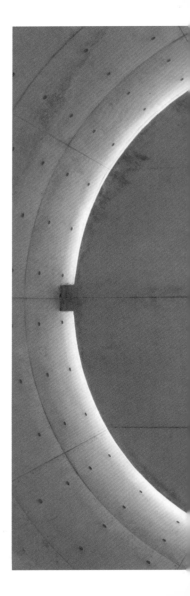

These solid walls – which measure up to 3m (10 ft) deep – have the primitive heaviness of those found in a medieval castle. The stained glass windows in the walls' inclined apertures are positioned at varying depths, softening the southerly light. Chapel of Notre-Dame-du-Haut, Ronchamp, France, 1954, Le Corbusier

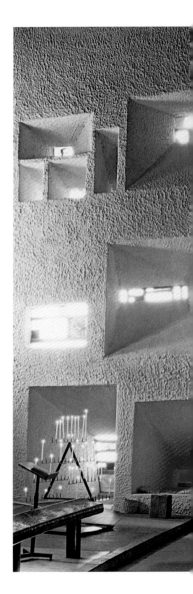

This postgraduate school is a bold 35m (115 ft) cube that dwarfs the neighbouring residential buildings. The unusual fenestration features three different sizes of window, scattered seemingly randomly over the facade, disguising the floor plan. Folkwang University of the Arts (formerly Zollverein School of Management and Design), Essen, Germany, 2006, SANAA

◀ This chapel appears to be part of the terrain. Its main room is elevated to afford views above a giant boulder and to allow the equinoctial sun to set precisely behind the altar cross. Sunset Chapel, Acapulco, Mexico, 2011, BNKR Arquitectura

Wright used the immense strength of reinforced concrete for the tall tree-like columns of the Great Workroom. The 250 workers shared a single, vast windowless room, lit from above by a glazed ceiling. Johnson Wax Headquarters, Racine, Wisconsin, USA, 1936, Frank Lloyd Wright

Irregularly positioned columns encourage contemplative navigation of
this room in a crematorium. The calming tree-like arrangement reflects the
building's position in a small forest on
the edge of Berlin. Baumschulenweg
Crematorium, Berlin, Germany, 1999,
Axel Schultes and Charlotte Frank

Best known as a revolutionary bridge designer, Maillart endlessly experimented with concrete. This 12m (39 ft) high temporary exhibition space was made of reinforced concrete. Its invisibly ribbed walls measured just 6cm (2⅜ in) thick. The hall was an inverted catenary arch, sharing the same shape as a rope hung between two points. This mathematical path has great strength and is often used to produce an arch which is the same thickness at the base as at the apex. Cement Hall, Zurich, Switzerland, 1939 (demolished 1940), Robert Maillart

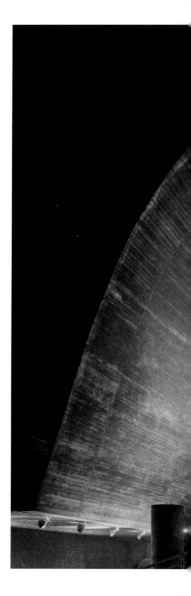

Erich Mendelsohn was one of a group of architects who fled Nazi Germany in the 1930s. His competition-winning seafront pavilion was the first Modernist building in Britain. Today it still provides a series of spaces for public use. De La Warr Pavilion, Bexhill-on Sea, UK, 1935, Erich Mendelsohn and Serge Chermayeff

This vast exhibition hall was built shortly after World War II. Its 96m (315 ft) long waveform roof was precast, and the entire building constructed in just 10 months. Nervi focused on the engineering aspects of his buildings. He considered their beauty a consequence of technical rigour, rather than an aim in itself.

Exhibition Building, Turin, Italy, 1949, Pier Luigi Nervi

◀ This railway viaduct skirts the town of Sembrancher – crossing a river and two main roads – and connects each side of the valley floor. Utilitarian and spare yet elegant, this long low bridge shows both fragility and strength and an effortless quality that approaches weightlessness. Sembrancher Railway Bridge, Sembrancher, Switzerland, 1953, Alexandre Sarrasin

A perfect concrete cube encloses a smaller cube, mysteriously skewed in relation to the first. Muted sunshine enters through carved light wells. Holy Rosary Catholic Church, St. Amant, Louisiana, USA, 2004, Trahan Architects

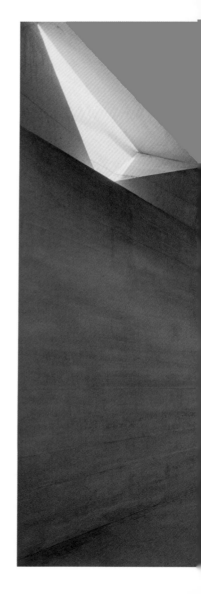

Hemmed in by suburban Yokohama, this building exploits a south-facing skylight to fill the space with light without being overlooked. Inside, the rooflines help define the open-plan rooms without closing them off completely. House in Kohoku, Yokohama, Japan, 2008, Torafu

MASS

◀ Neatly fitted into a small plot, this three-storey home incorporates a dance studio as part of an open middle floor that also doubles as a living and dining room. The starkly minimalist facade is tempered by a corner light box that is continued as a skylight along the full width of the building, flooding the house with light. Dancing Living House, Tokyo, Japan, 2009, A.L.X.

This innovative modular structure was the first capsule building in the world. Each 4 x 2.5 m (13 x 8 ft) converted shipping container is attached to a concrete tower by four bolts and fitted out as a tiny self-contained living space or office. Nakagin Capsule Tower, Tokyo, Japan, 1972, Kisho Kurokawa

This 30 m (98 ft) long, 12 m (39 ft) wide in situ concrete block gives shade from the Brazilian sunshine and is a focal point leading visitors towards a subterranean plaza. The weight and mass of this giant slab has an appropriately sculptural quality. Brazilian Museum of Sculpture, São Paulo, Brazil, 1988, Paulo Mendes da Rocha

This wedge-shaped dam measures 14m (46 ft) wide at the top and 200m (656 ft) wide at the base. The original design for the facade had unbalanced outlet houses and massive eagles on the roadway towers, all of which contrasted with the modern image the builders wanted to project. Kaufmann's solution was a comparatively simple Art Deco relief featuring motifs of the local Native American tribes, Navajo and Pueblo. Hoover Dam, Black Canyon, bordering Arizona and Nevada, USA, 1936, Frank Crowe with detailing by Gordon Kaufmann

The colour of the Centre's concrete, mixed with brick and local stone, mimics that of the surrounding earth, and its wavy walls are redolent of the ploughed agricultural land on which it sits. All of this is appropriate for a gallery displaying work that responds to the landscape. Centre for Art and Nature, Huesca, Spain, 2006, Rafael Moneo

The surface of this severe, object-like building demonstrates the rich texture and colouring that can be achieved by combining local stone in the concrete mixture. Dutch Reformed Church, Rijsenhout, Netherlands, 2006, Claus en Kaan

'Most parking garages look like office buildings without glass,' said Rudolph when asked about this city centre car park, adding that he wanted the building to 'look like it belonged to the automobile and its movement'. The building stretches for 270m (886 ft). Rudolph's original plan had it extending three times as far and traversing a motorway. Temple Street Parking Garage, New Haven, Connecticut, USA, 1962, Paul Rudolph

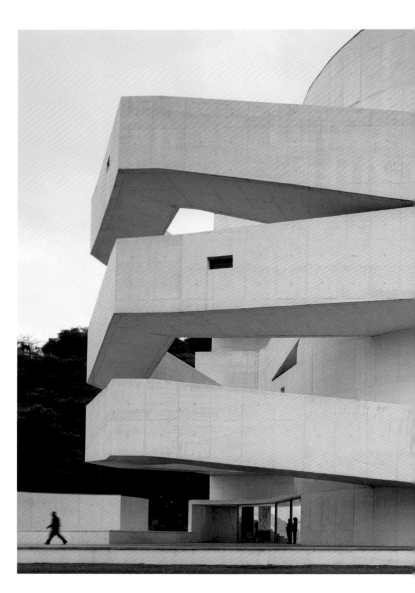

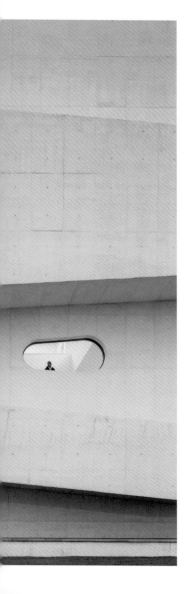

Like a New York Guggenheim Museum pulled inside out, the finger-like walkways of the Iberê Camargo Foundation encourage visitors to circulate around the gallery and give the building both a strong identity and a shaded forecourt. Iberê Camargo Foundation, Porto Alegre, Brazil, 2008, Álvaro Siza

This building houses a kiln for a family of ceramicists. The Japanese cedar formwork of this in situ concrete box was reused as flooring, ceiling panels, doors and even interior cabinets.

Miwa-Gama Storage and Display Building, Hagi, Japan, 2002, Hiroshi Sambuichi

This collection of 24 cubes – each measuring 3m³ (106 cu ft), having its own function, and defined internally by fixed or moving walls – has a steel structure with concrete or glass panels. The glass panels shown in this photograph (the third on the top floor and the first, fourth and fifth on the ground floor) are fitted with concrete-coloured blinds. Villa in Beroun, Beroun, Czech Republic, 2004, HSH Architects

◀ The interior spaces of this government building are treated with the same bold geometry and calm monumentality as its exterior spaces. National Assembly Building, Dhaka, Bangladesh, 1983, Louis I Kahn

Neviges has been a pilgrimage destination since the seventeenthcentury. This church is situated on the highest point of the site and is reached via a processional approach that includes accommodation for pilgrims. Most churches reach towards the heavens, but this ruggedly crystalline roofscape seems austerely grounded rather than extending skywards. Pilgrimage Church, Neviges, Germany, 1972, Gottfried Böhm

Planning permission for this redeveloped barn in a protected historical area was granted on the condition that the building envelope would be exactly the same as that it replaced. Red iron oxide was added to the concrete to give a rusty appearance.
Bardill Studio, Scharans, Switzerland, 2007, Valerio Olgiati

This simple exterior conceals a series of different spaces designed to make the medical facility feel welcoming and encourage voluntary blood donations. Costs were kept, in the words of the architect, 'abysmally low', by fabricating doors, windows and much of the furniture locally. Large pieces of furniture, such as the reception desk and conference table, were made with in situ concrete.
Prathama Blood Centre, Ahmedabad, India, 2000, Matharoo Associates

To visit this gallery you must borrow a key from an osteria in the nearby village. There is just one door to enter and exit, and skylights provide the only light source in an otherwise windowless structure. La Congiunta, Giornico, Switzerland, 1992, Peter Märkli

These sculptural, windowless concrete walls face the motorway, while on the opposite side glass facades face landscaped grounds. Concrete comes in many different finishes, but is never a totally sterile material: it contains imperfections, air holes and bits of grit or scratches. Unlike glass or steel it shows its history. These qualities prevent large blank walls like these becoming mundane. The Pyramids, Indianapolis, Indiana, USA, 1972, Roche-Dinkeloo and Associates

Part of a new public square, this concert hall's unconventional upturned-fist shape and large apertures draw people in with all the appeal of a landed spacecraft. Casa da Música, Porto, Portugal, 2005, Rem Koolhass

PRESENCE

◀ This sculptural work divides Mexico City's main motorway. While each tower is consistently triangular in plan, the whole arrangement appears different depending on the viewer's direction of transit. The shifting shapes and colours create an engaging and ambiguous monument. Satellite Towers, Mexico City, Mexico, 1957, Luis Barragán with Mathias Goeritz

The Vitra Fire Station's exploding shards of concrete convey movement and energy. This angular building leads visitors into its dynamic folds, leaning walls and strange in-between spaces. Vitra Fire Station, Weil am Rhein, Germany, 1994, Zaha Hadid

◀ Built on an ancient sacred site just two years after his pragmatic and linear Unité d'Habitation (347), Le Corbusier's hilltop chapel has a unique and unplaceable style that manages to make it seem both ancient and modern at the same time. The walls are finished with distinctively rough sprayed concrete – meaning liquid concrete is pumped through a hose directly onto the wall. Chapel of Notre-Dame-du-Haut, Ronchamp, France, 1955, Le Corbusier

This building on a narrow site quietly and austerely shuts out the neighbour hood. Inside the austerity is even more extreme – all that is visible are the wall, trees and sky. Ando embraced the sensuality of exposed concrete and was a pioneer in using it for residential projects. Nakayama House, Nara, Japan, 1964, Tadao Ando

Architect Patrick Hodgkinson had intended the Brunswick Centre to be built in brick and painted cream like the neighbouring stuccoed terraces of Bloomsbury. Instead, council cutbacks resulted in an unintended Brutalist construction of exposed concrete, until it was finally painted during renovations that Hodgkinson oversaw in 2006. Brunswick Centre, London, UK, 1972, Patrick Hodgkinson

One of Ando's earliest projects, this small Osaka house is squeezed into a narrow road in a dense neighbour hood. The stark, blank facade gives way to a slim domestic interior divided into three equal spaces, with the middle section open to the sky in an attempt to 'contact with light, air, rain and other natural elements', according to Ando. Azuma House, Osaka, Japan, 1976, Tadao Ando

◀ This structure replaces a neo-Gothic church destroyed during World War II. Its entire interior and exterior is constructed from reinforced concrete. The V-shaped wall elements are conjoined by tall stained glass windows, which have a total area of 500 m² (5,382 sq ft). Church of Notre-Dame de Royan, Royan, France, 1958, Guillaume Gillet and Marc Hébrard

This church is one of the earliest in the world – and the first in Switzerland – to use exposed concrete. The main part of the church relates closely to the surrounding residential buildings and sits flush with them away from the street, but the belfry – at 62 m (203 ft) high – is three times higher. St Anthony's Church, Basel, Switzerland, 1927, Karl Moser

◀ Built over 23 years, the National Assembly Building is the focus of a 197 acre (80 hectare) plot – one of the largest legislative sites in the world. Thin white marble lines give scale to the building and pattern to the facades. That one of the poorest countries in the world created a monumental building of quietly spoken grandeur with simple and cheap materials is re-markable. National Assembly Building, Dhaka, Bangladesh, 1982, Louis I Kahn

Three cantilevered volumes provide space for three separate auditoria or combine into one volume with seating for 1,000. The building is distinctly inward looking, shutting out the hostile city. Melnikov described its exterior as 'tensed muscle'. Rusakov Workers' Club, Moscow, Russia, 1928, Konstantin Melnikov

It is hard to overstate how radical this building must have appeared in 1924. While the ground floor is divided conventionally, the first floor is open-plan but uses sliding screens to break up the space. Rietveld wanted to construct the building in concrete, but the steel for reinforcement was difficult to source in the interwar years, and it proved too expensive. In the end, the only elements built in concrete were the foundations and balconies.

Schröder House, Utrecht, Netherlands, 1924, Gerrit Rietveld

◀ Responding to the loss of a row of Victorian terrace houses in the East End of London, Whiteread filled an archetypal empty house with liquid concrete and then peeled away the exterior of the house. The resulting artwork is a combination of architecture and sculpture, and of the familiar and the strange. A critic described it as 'one of the most extraordinary and imaginative sculptures created by an English artist this century'. House, London, UK, 1993 (demolished 1994), Rachel Whiteread

Entry to this cathedral is via a ramp that is set away from the building and that descends to the below-ground-level nave. This invisible entrance means the main structure is unencumbered by doors. Stained glass connects the 16 ribs – a sculptural crown of thorns. Cathedral of Brasília, Brasília, Brazil, 1970, Oscar Niemeyer

◀ Sydney Harbour's iconic structure could not have been created in any material but reinforced concrete, although its famous sails are clad in white ceramic tiles. Utzon was interested in architecture that resembled natural forms. The unprecedented design may have been influenced by his fascination with the wing structures of birds, or by sound or sea waves.
Sydney Opera House, Sydney, Australia, 1973, Jørn Utzon

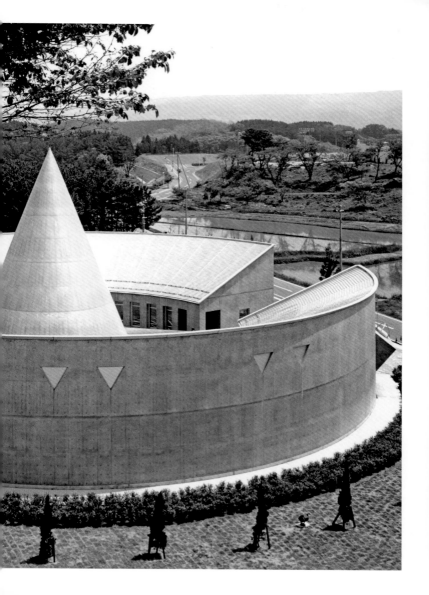

◀ Nobu Shirase was a Japanese explorer of the Antarctic. The outer ring of this building contains an exhibition of Shirase's expedition designed to educate and inspire a new generation of explorers, while the inner cone is a memorial hall used for events. Memorial Hall for Shirase, Akita, Japan, 1991, Kisho Kurokaw

Like medieval battlements, these 'flak towers' were built by the Luftwaffe to withstand Allied air raids and to shelter civilians in Berlin, Hamburg and Vienna. Some had walls up to 3.5m (12 ft) thick. They were considered virtually impenetrable, and both the RAF and Soviet forces avoided them. Flakturm VII, Vienna, Austria, 1940, Friedrich Tamms

A circular canopy provides shade and shelter during the day and doubles as a beacon when illuminated at night. Jacobsen is best known as a chair designer; his plywood stacking chairs have become ubiquitous. This roof echoes their pleasingly simple forms. Skovshoved Petrol Station, Copenhagen, Denmark, 1936, Arne Jacobsen

Le Corbusier's celebrated five points of architecture (columns on the ground floor, open-plan interiors, a facade free from supports, ribbon windows and roof gardens) are most succinctly illustrated in this building, a private house outside Paris. These five points are strongly associated with the materials that made them achievable, such as steel, glass and, especially, reinforced concrete. Villa Savoye, Poissy, France, 1931, Le Corbusier and Pierre Jeanneret

Overlooking a popular beach, this hotel
incorporates a cinema, dance hall,
café and swimming pool. Bedrooms,
many with views across the Black
Sea, are situated on the perimeter.
The building's strange shape attracted
the attention of the Pentagon, which
initially mistook it for a rocket launcher.
Druzhba Holiday Centre, Yalta, Ukraine,
1984, Igor Vasilevsky

Dwarfing neighbouring buildings, the main block is attached to a service tower every three floors. The tower incorporates lifts, stairs, refuse chutes and the boiler house, and it is also a home for nesting kestrels.
Trellick Tower, London, UK, 1972, Ernö Goldfinger

◀ Cylindrical volumes are the trunks from which round overhanging balconies sprout at the top of this mixed-use, but predominantly residential, building. The building was conceived in white (hence the name White Towers), but ultimately its budget did not stretch to include the powdered marble required to turn the concrete mix white. Torres Blancas Apartment Building, Madrid, Spain, 1969, Francisco Javier Sáenz de Oiza

At the start of the 1960s Chicago's citizens were increasingly heading to the suburbs. This project aimed to reverse the movement by providing convenient living in the centre of the city. At 179m (587 ft) tall, Marina City was then the tallest residential project in the world, and its corncob shape a confident but delicate presence on the Chicago skyline. Marina City, Chicago, Illinois, USA, 1964, Bertrand Goldberg

◀ Tange's mother died in a bombing on the same day that the atomic bomb was dropped on Hiroshima. This, coupled with his schooling in Hiroshima, gave him an affinity with the city. Integrating traditional Japanese architecture with Western Modernism, Tange created a building that humbly welcomes the international community. Peace Memorial and Museum, Hiroshima, Japan, 1955, Kenzo Tange

Torre Velasca took inspiration from medieval castles and bell towers, giving the expanded upper stories an unusual and distinctive profile. Torre Velasca, Milan, Italy, 1958, BBPR

Much of the character of this building, an imposing and alien structure, comes from the ship-like ribbon windows that reflect the often intensely colourful California sky. The building houses a university library, and some students have noted that the fantastic views from it are too distracting. Geisel Library, San Diego, California, USA, 1970, William Pereira

SCALE

◄ One of the most influential concrete buildings ever made, Unité has inspired many great copies, and many poor ones too. Most of the apartments – accessed via internal 'streets' – have double-height living rooms and traverse the building from east to west. Le Corbusier envisioned a self-contained community, such that the building contains shops, a restaurant and a hotel for visiting guests. The roof terrace incorporates a running track, open-air theatre, crèche and sports hall. Unité d'Habitation, Marseille, France, 1952, Le Corbusier

Replacing a series of old churches – and therefore required to house their congregations – this monumental conical cathedral has a capacity for 20,000 people in a single vast room measuring 75 m (246 ft) high. Metropolitan Cathedral, Rio de Janeiro, Brazil, 1979, Edgar de Oliveira da Fonseca

A grid of indented window frames on a gently curved tower facade gives this large building a sense of scale. Centre Point stood empty for over a decade after its completion, leading to the emergence of conspiracy theories. One theory was that the building – then the only entirely sealed and air-conditioned building in London – was really a secret government office able to survive nuclear or biological attacks. Centre Point, London, UK, 1966, Richard Seifert

Ascetic exposed concrete contributes considerable austerity and gravitas to the interior of this church. Natural light enters from a pair of slots that run up the walls and across the ceiling and that cross at right angles to one another. St Mary's Cathedral, Tokyo, Japan, 1964, Kenzo Tange

This extraordinary church was inspired by the basalt lava flows of the Icelandic landscape. Despite its monumental scale it demonstrates the unexpectedly sensuous quality that concrete can have. Hallgrímskirkja, Reykjavik, Iceland, 1986, Guðjón Samúelsson

◀ The 35 acre (14 hectare) site of this housing complex in the centre of London was almost entirely destroyed by bombing in World War II and remained a wasteland until building began in 1965. Within the site there are shared amenities, open spaces and a lake. Three 42-storey towers – triangular in plan with distinctive upturned balconies – dominate the estate. Barbican Estate, London, UK, 1976, Chamberlin, Powell and Bon

When completed in 1913, the Centennial Hall was the largest dome in the world, with a diameter of 65m (213 ft) and seating for 18,000. The dome was so huge that some visitors feared its collapse and were too afraid to enter it. Centennial Hall, Wrocław, Poland, 1913, Max Berg

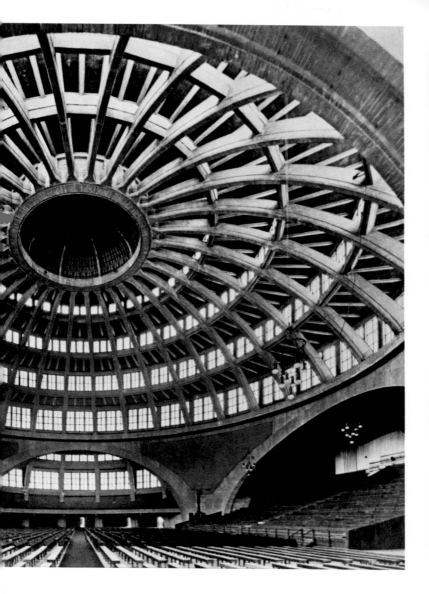

The huge, sweeping, fluted roof of CNIT is the largest enclosed unsupported concrete span in the world. Each corner is 218 m (715 ft) apart. It was one of the first buildings of the major Parisian business district La Défense. Centre National des Industries et Techniques (CNIT), Paris, France, 1958, Bernard Zehrfuss, Robert Edouard Camelot and Jean de Mailly

These apartment buildings were the beginning of a three-stage project completed over 17 years. This original site had a 60 degree incline. Rather than build a tower away from the hill, Ando chose to create a low-rise structure that followed the landscape and that kept each building close to nature. Rokko Housing Project, Kobe, Japan, 1999, Tadao Ando

Concrete buildings can sometimes present an impervious and dominating presence, but even this gigantic 152 m (499 ft) high tower was toppled by dynamite in less than a minute. Trojan Nuclear Power Plant, Rainier, Oregon, USA, 1975 (demolished 2006), Bechtel

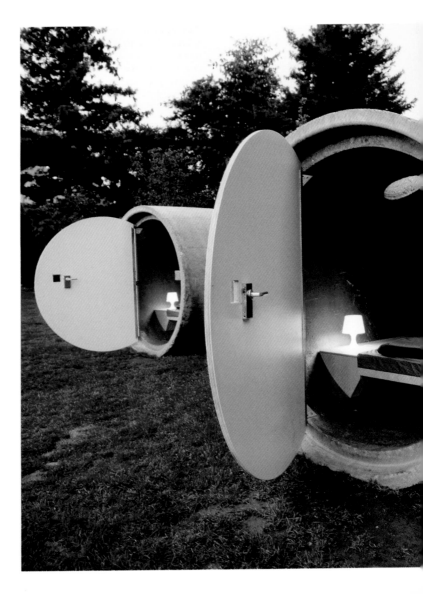

This modular hotel reimagines industrial-size pipes as cheap capsule hotels. Guests sleep in the tubes and share nearby bathroom facilities. It is difficult to imagine a simpler or more economical form for a room. Das Parkhotel, Ottensheim, Austria, 2005, Andreas Strauss

This organic and fluid family home deliberately turns away from the road and cramped suburbs, and inward towards an internal courtyard. Truss Wall House, Tokyo, Japan, 1993, Ushida Findlay

The delicacy of this private house is emphasized by its position in an undistinguished Tokyo suburb. Its hidden apertures and blank walls might appear unwelcoming on a larger building; instead, its diminutive scale makes these friendly and unthreatening.
Reflection of Mineral, Tokyo, Japan, 2006, Yasuhiro Yamashita

The Three Gorges Dam contains the largest power station in the world. It was built to supply 10 per cent of China's energy needs, but demand has increased so much since its conception that it now contributes just three per cent. This view is of ship locks to one side of the dam. The dam wall itself is nearly 2.4 km (1.5 miles) long, which created a reservoir 595 km (370 miles) long – about the distance from London to Frankfurt. The reservoir flooded 1,300 archaeological sites and caused the relocation of over one million people. Three Gorges Dam, Hubei Province, China, 2008

Following the contours of the hill it stands on, the site of this curving 260 m (853 ft) long apartment block incorporates many public amenities, such as swimming pools, a school and a theatre. Pedregulho Estate, Rio de Janeiro, Brazil, 1952, Affonso Eduardo Reidy

▶ Built following a series of major floods, this vast underground waterway is the largest in the world. One part of the complex is this 177 m (581 ft) long, 25 m (82 ft) tall water tank. From here 181,500 kg (200 tons) of water a second can be pumped away into the distant Edogawa River. Metropolitan Area Outer Underground Discharge Channel, Saitama, Japan, 1992

Index

Page numbers in *italics* refer to illustrations.

The glossary is incorporated within the captions throughout the book. To use, search for entries in **bold**. Page numbers in **bold** refer to key definitions.

Endnotes

p22 Kostof, Spiro, *A History of Architecture, Settings and Rituals*, Oxford University Press, 1985. p740
p27 Official Wotruba Church website www.georgenberg.at
p32 Candela, Felix, Shell Structure Development, *The Canadian Architect*, 1967. Vol. 12 p33
p36 Heyer, Paul, *Architects on Architecture*, The Penguin Press, 1967. p307
p44 Jones, Cranston, *Architecture Today and Tomorrow*, McGraw-Hill, 1961. p226
p56 Botta, Mario, *Architetture 1960–1985*, Electa, 1985.

50 Henschel, Klaus, *The Einstein Tower: An Intertexture of Dynamic Construction, Relativity, Theory and Astronomy*, Stanford University Press, 1997. p59

53 Torroja, Eduardo, *Philosophy of Structures*, University of California Press, 1967. p309

56 Muschamp, Herbert, Stay of Execution for a Dazzling Airline Terminal, *The New York Times*, Architecture View, 6 November 1994.

04 Potie, Philippe, *Le Corbusier: The Convent at La Tourette*, Birkhäuser Verlag, 2001. p7

07 Treiber, Daniel, *Frank Lloyd Wright*, Birkhäuser Architecture, 2008. p72

46 Koolhaas, Rem, OMA + Rem Koolhaas 1987–1998, *El Croquis*, 1998. p134

52 Sharp, Dennis, *Twentieth Century Architecture: A Visual History*, Images Publishing, 2002. p281

64 Villanova Artigas, João Batista, *Vilanova Artigas*, Instituto Lina Bo e PM Bardi, 1997. p101

64 *Toyo Ito & Associates press release: Meiso no Mori*, Issue 10

08 Perrone, Carlos, *São Paulo Por Dentro: Um Guia Panorâmico de Arquitetura*, Editora SENAC São Paulo, 1999.

10 SANAA press release: *Opening of Rolex Learning Center Press Information*, 17 February 2010.

24 Tadao Ando lecture, 2 June 2011, Royal Institution

33 Coleman, Nathaniel, *Utopias and Architecture*, Routledge, 2005. p128

34 Luis Barragán's Laureate Acceptance Speech, Dumbarton Oaks, Washington DC, 1980.

74 Harris, Neil, *Cultural Excursions: Marketing Appetites and Cultural Tastes in Modern America*, University of Chicago Press, 1990.

88 Matharoo Associates press release: *Prathama Blood Center*, Ahmedabad, 2000.

06 Frampton, Kenneth, *Tadao Ando: Buildings Projects Writings*, Rizzoli, 1988. p26

14 Gray Read, Alice, Doo, Peter and Burton, Joseph, *Architecture and Visual Perception*, University of Pennsylvania, 1983. p108

20 Kester, Grant H., *Conversation Pieces: Community and Communication in Modern Art*, University of California Press, 2004. p18

otographic Credits

Arcaid Images/Alamy 123; A.L.X./Kouicha Torimura 263; g-images 143, 359; akg-images/VIEW Pictures Ltd 228; nat, Guillaume 308–309; Ano, Daici 261, 279; Archipicture 6; The Architectural Archives, University of Pennsylvania, oto by Nurer Ramhan Khan 312–313; Architektur, courtesy Kunstmuseum Liechtenstein 87; © ARS, NY and DACS, ndon 2011. Courtesy S C Johnson and Son inc 247; The Art stitute of Chicago. Courtesy of Geoff Goldberg 339; stermann, Aric 103; Baan, Iwan 192–193; Baier Bischofberger chitects 81; © Barbosa & Guimarães 59; © 2011 Barragan undation, Birsfelden, Switzerland/ProLitteris/DACS. otograph by Armando Salas Portugal 187; Berrel Berrel autler 212–213; Binet, Hélène 84–85, 93, 175, 299; Bitter, Jan ; BluesyPete 373; Bognar, Botond 307; Brink, Barbara 239; yant, Richard/Arcaid Images 120–121; Bureau of clamation, Lower Colorado Regional Office 268; Campo eza, Alberto 133; Archivo Carmen Portinho 374; © Charles, artin 231; Claus en Kaan Architecten 272; Collection Centraal useum, Utrecht © DACS 2011 317; Conde Nast 97; Conley, n 191; Corbis images 37, 205, 207; Crawford, Vanessa 106; AC Università degli Studi di Parma Sezione Fotografia, hivio Vasari 45; Davies, John 318–319; Eero Saarinen

Collection, Manuscripts and Archives, Yale University Library 67; Einzig, Richard/Arcaid Images 356–357; FAU-USP 51, 163; Museum of Finnish Architecture 73; Finotti, Leonardo 38, 201, 267, 349; © FLC/DACS, 2011 105, 220, 331, 347; © FLC/DACS, 2011, Photographer: Olivier Martin–Gambier 232; Fonds Parent. SIAF/Cité de l'architecture et du patrimoine/Archives d'architecture du XXe siècle 30–31; Fonds Perret frères. CNAM/SIAF/CAPA, Archives d'architecture du XXe siècle/Auguste Perret/UFSE/SAIF/année 55; Fonds Simon Boussiron. SIAF/Cité de l'architecture et du patrimoine/Archives d'architecture du XXe siècle 361; courtesy Garcia Rubio, Justo 53; Gempelar, Alexander 109; Getty images/Hulton Archive 340–341; Grundy, Paul 351; gta Archives/ETH Zurich 251, 311; Guerra, Fernando 125; Guerra, Fernando, FG+SG Fotografia 276; Guidi, Guido 102; Gutiérrez Marcos, Javier 62; Halbe, Roland 28, 76, 129, 216–217, 300–301; Hall, Steve © Hedrich Blessing 149; Hirai, Hiroyuki 177; Hiroshi Kobayashi, © shikenchiku/Arcaid Images 303; HSH Architects 281; Huthmacher, Werner 249; Courtesy Institution of Civil Engineers 33; Ishiguro Photographic Institute 179; Ishimoto, Yasuhiro 131; Jauréguiberry, Xavier de 285; Kapellos, Alexandre 91; Kegge, Bas 101; Kennedy, Philip 329; Kida, Katsuhisa 369; Kok, Pedro 99; Kon, Nelson 40–41, 209; Lang, Erwin 225; Lavine, Michael 47; Leeb, Wolf 26; Lejtreger, Rafael 48–49; Leng, James 363; Lins, Marc 21; Linsi, Martin 256–257; Lohmann, Doris 135; Lopez, Diego 336–337; Malagamba, Duccio 183, 270; Matharoo Associates 289; Matsuoka, Mitsuo 181; Meurs, Paul 321; Minnesota Historical Society 71; Instituto Moreira Salles 95; Morikawa, Noboru 168–169; Mudford, Grant 117; Murai, Osamu 141; © Museum of London/photographer Mike Seaborne 335; S.W. Newbery 153; © Joe Nishizawa 376–377; Norihiko Dan and Associates 79; Norsworthy, Scott 115; North Carolina State Archives 34–35; Ohashi, Tomio, Courtesy Kisho Kurakawa Architect and Associates 265, 324–325; Archive Olgiati 287; OMA 295; ORCH Studio Fotografico 282–283; Ottenstein, David 275; Palma, Cristobal 145; Perry, Curtis Gregory 364; Quijano, Augusto 113; Realgrün Landschaftarchitekten 173; Rewal, Raj 185; RIBA Library Photographs Collection 61, 111, 150–151, 227, 253, 255, 315, 343; RIBA Library Photographs Collection/Architectural Press Archive 197; RIBA Library Photographs Collection/John Donat 305; RIBA Library Photographs Collection/Duccio Malagamba 158–159; Richter, Christian 161; Richter, Christian courtesy of Diener & Diener 138–139; Courtesy of Kevin Roche John Dinkeloo and Associates 292; Sarthou, Julien 355; Scarpi, Filippo 157; Schezen, Robert/Agenzia Fotografica Luisa Ricciaini, Milan 237; Shinkenchiku-sha 69; Silverman, Stephen 235; © The Solomon R Guggenheim Foundation, New York. Photograph by Robert E. Mates 23; Courtesy of Souto de Moura 219; Spiluttini, Margherita 89, 291, 327; © SPK/photo Ute Zscharnt for David Chipperfield Architects 137; Stark, James 65; Archivio Storico Fiat 171; Suarez, Esteban 244–245; Südwestdeutsches Archiv für Architektur und Ingenieurbau Karlsruhe, Photo Horstheinz Neuendorff 129; Sugioka, Ichiro 75; Superstock 215; Suzuki, Hisao 118, 199, 211; Sydney Opera House 322–323; Thomas Mayer Archive 243; Archivo Torroja, CEHOPU-CEDEX 43; Toyo Ito Associates 165; Trahan Architects 259; UC San Diego Libraries 345; Veytia, Eduardo Torres 297; Vyacheslav Argenberg © VascoPlanet 333; Weinreb, Matthew 241; Werlemann, Hans 147; Yoshida, Makoto courtesy of Atelier Tekuto 371; Yusheng, Liao 323, 353; Zanetta, Alo 57; Zollinger, Daniel 202–203; ZSL 25;

Phaidon Press Limited
Regent's Wharf
All Saints Street
London N1 9PA

Phaidon Press Inc.
65 Bleecker Street
New York, NY 10012

phaidon.com

First published 2012
© 2012 Phaidon Press Limited
This edition first published 2017
Reprinted 2019
© 2017 Phaidon Press Limited

ISBN 978 0 7148 7515 6

A CIP catalogue record for this book
is available from the British Library
and the Library of Congress.

Commissioning Editor: Emilia Terragni
Project Editor: Taahir Husain
Production Controller: Sarah Kramer
Design: William Hall

Printed in China